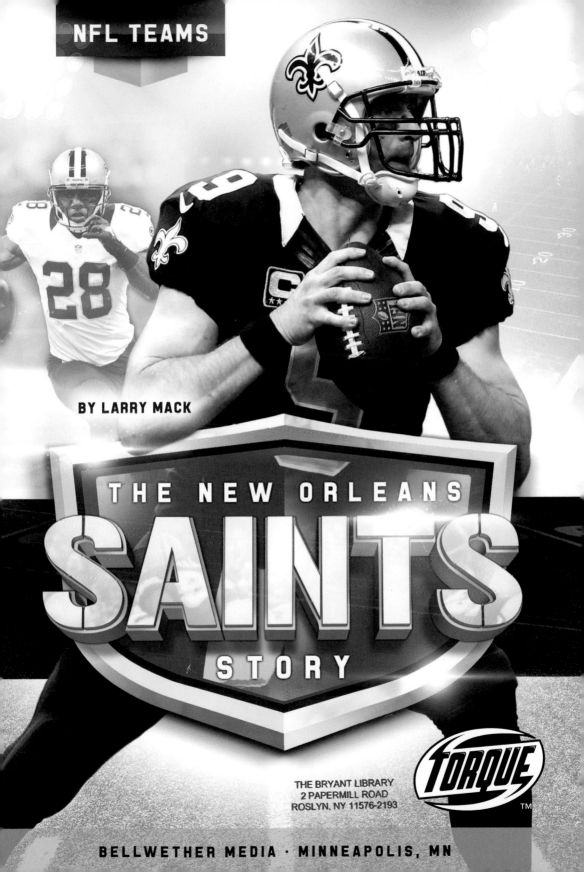

BY LARRY MACK

THE NEW ORLEANS
SAINTS
STORY

TORQUE
TM

BELLWETHER MEDIA · MINNEAPOLIS, MN

Are you ready to take it to the extreme? Torque books thrust you into the action-packed world of sports, vehicles, mystery, and adventure. These books may include dirt, smoke, fire, and chilling tales. **WARNING**: read at your own risk.

This edition first published in 2017 by Bellwether Media, Inc.

No part of this publication may be reproduced in whole or in part without written permission of the publisher. For information regarding permission, write to Bellwether Media, Inc., Attention: Permissions Department, 5357 Penn Avenue South, Minneapolis, MN 55419.

Library of Congress Cataloging-in-Publication Data

Names: Mack, Larry.
Title: The New Orleans Saints Story / by Larry Mack.
Description: Minneapolis, MN : Bellwether Media, Inc., 2017. | Series:
   Torque: NFL Teams | Includes bibliographical references and index. |
   Audience: Ages: 7-12. | Audience: Grades: 3 through 7.
Identifiers: LCCN 2016009315 | ISBN 9781626173743 (hardcover : alk. paper)
Subjects: LCSH: New Orleans Saints (Football team)–History–Juvenile literature.
Classification: LCC GV956.N366 M32 2017 | DDC 796.332/640976335–dc23
LC record available at http://lccn.loc.gov/2016009315

Printed in the United States of America, North Mankato, MN.

TABLE OF CONTENTS

Saints players pace the sidelines. **Super Bowl** 44 is the biggest game of their lives. They are in the last quarter of the game against the Indianapolis Colts.

Pierre Thomas

4

The Colts lead by one point. They try for a field goal and miss. New Orleans gets the ball and marches up the field.

Drew Brees

Quarterback Drew Brees throws to Jeremy Shockey. Touchdown! With a two-point conversion, the Saints lead by seven.

The Colts storm back toward their goal line. Suddenly, Tracy Porter **intercepts** their pass! He runs the ball up the field for another touchdown. The Saints win their first Super Bowl!

Tracy Porter

SCORING TERMS

END ZONE
the area at each end of a football field; a team scores by entering the opponent's end zone with the football.

EXTRA POINT
a score that occurs when a kicker kicks the ball between the opponent's goal posts after a touchdown is scored; 1 point.

FIELD GOAL
a score that occurs when a kicker kicks the ball between the opponent's goal posts; 3 points.

SAFETY
a score that occurs when a player on offense is tackled behind his own goal line; 2 points for defense.

TOUCHDOWN
a score that occurs when a team crosses into its opponent's end zone with the football; 6 points.

TWO-POINT CONVERSION
a score that occurs when a team crosses into its opponent's end zone with the football after scoring a touchdown; 2 points.

In 2016, the New Orleans Saints marked 50 seasons in the National Football League (NFL). They play in a spirited city and have had star players.

8

Like all teams, the Saints have had ups and downs. They celebrate good times, such as winning an NFL Championship.

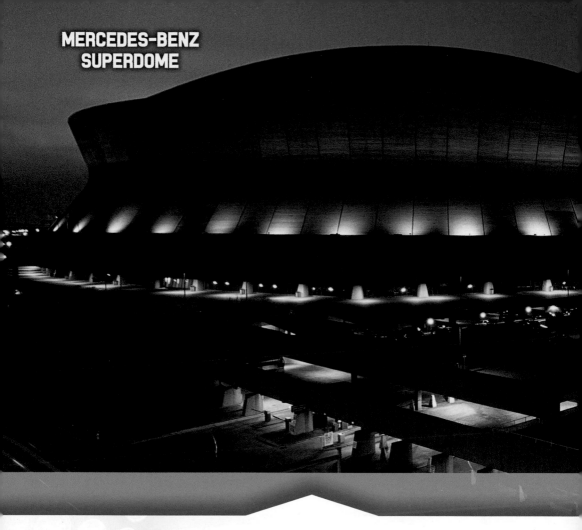

The Saints play their home games in the Mercedes-Benz Superdome. The Superdome is 273 feet (83 meters) tall from floor to ceiling.

New Orleans is a popular city to visit. Because of this, the Superdome hosts many sporting events. In 2013, it hosted its seventh Super Bowl.

SHELTER FROM THE STORM

Hurricane Katrina hit New Orleans in 2005. The Superdome sheltered 30,000 people.

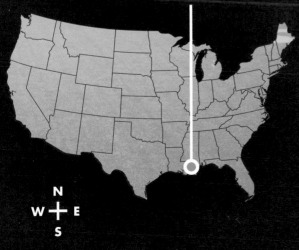

NEW ORLEANS, LOUISIANA

N
W E
S

The Saints play in the NFL's National Football **Conference** (NFC). For many years, they were part of the NFC West **Division**. In 2002, however, the Saints moved to the NFC South. The Atlanta Falcons are the Saints' biggest division **rival**.

NFL DIVISIONS

AFC

AFC NORTH

	BALTIMORE RAVENS		CINCINNATI BENGALS
	CLEVELAND BROWNS		PITTSBURGH STEELERS

AFC EAST

	BUFFALO BILLS		MIAMI DOLPHINS
	PATRIOTS		NEW YORK JETS

AFC SOUTH

	TEXANS		INDIANAPOLIS COLTS
	JACKSONVILLE JAGUARS		TENNESSEE TITANS

AFC WEST

	DENVER BRONCOS		CHIEFS
	OAKLAND RAIDERS		SAN DIEGO CHARGERS

NFC

NFC NORTH

CHICAGO
BEARS

DETROIT
LIONS

GREEN BAY
PACKERS

MINNESOTA
VIKINGS

NFC EAST

DALLAS
COWBOYS

GIANTS

PHILADELPHIA
EAGLES

WASHINGTON
REDSKINS

NFC SOUTH

FALCONS

CAROLINA
PANTHERS

NEW ORLEANS
SAINTS

BUCCANEERS

NFC WEST

CARDINALS

LOS ANGELES
RAMS

SAN FRANCISCO
49ERS

SEATTLE
SEAHAWKS

The NFL awarded an **expansion team** to New Orleans in 1966. The Saints hit the field the next year.

Despite excited fans and talented players, the Saints lost often. Many coaches came and went. In 1986, the team hired a promising head coach named Jim Mora.

1967 season

Jim Mora

The next year, Coach Mora led the Saints to their first **winning record**. He was named NFL Coach of the Year. Mora stayed with the Saints for just over ten seasons.

Sean Payton

Today, Sean Payton coaches the team. He was hired in 2006 and guided the Saints to win Super Bowl 44!

TIMELINE

1966

Awarded as an NFL expansion team to New Orleans

1970

Celebrated kicker Tom Dempsey setting record for longest field goal, 63 yards

1975

Played first game in the Superdome

1967

Recorded first regular season win, beating the Philadelphia Eagles (31–24)

1978

Celebrated quarterback Archie Manning being named the NFC's MVP

1987

Posted first winning record with 12 wins and 3 losses

2000

Had first playoff victory, beating the St. Louis Rams (31-28)

2012

Celebrated quarterback Drew Brees being named NFL Offensive Player of the Year for the 2011 season

1988

Made first-ever playoff game, but lost to the Minnesota Vikings (10-44)

2010

Won Super Bowl 44, beating the Indianapolis Colts

31   FINAL SCORE   **17**

Quarterback Archie Manning was the Saints' first big star. He was **drafted** in 1971. Later on, William Roaf was an expert blocker on **offense**.

Peyton Manning

Archie Manning

LIKE FATHER, LIKE SONS
The Manning family loves football. Archie Manning is the father of famous NFL quarterbacks Peyton and Eli Manning.

Deuce McAllister

Eli Manning

Deuce McAllister was
big for the Saints, too.
The **running back** set
a team record for career
rushing yards.

On **defense**, Rickey Jackson made more than 100 **sacks** for the Saints. He is in the Pro Football Hall of Fame.

Two recent Saints stars are Drew Brees and Marques Colston. **Wide receiver** Colston set team records in receiving.

SAINT

TEAM GREATS

ARCHIE MANNING
QUARTERBACK
1971-1975, 1977-1982

RICKEY JACKSON
LINEBACKER
1981-1993

MORTEN ANDERSEN
KICKER
1982-1994

Rickey Jackson

KILLER KICKERS

Former kicker Morten Andersen is the NFL's highest scorer with 2,544 points. For 43 years, toeless Tom Dempsey held the record for longest-ever field goal.

WILLIAM ROAF
OFFENSIVE TACKLE
1993-2001

DEUCE McALLISTER
RUNNING BACK
2001-2008

DREW BREES
QUARTERBACK
2006-PRESENT

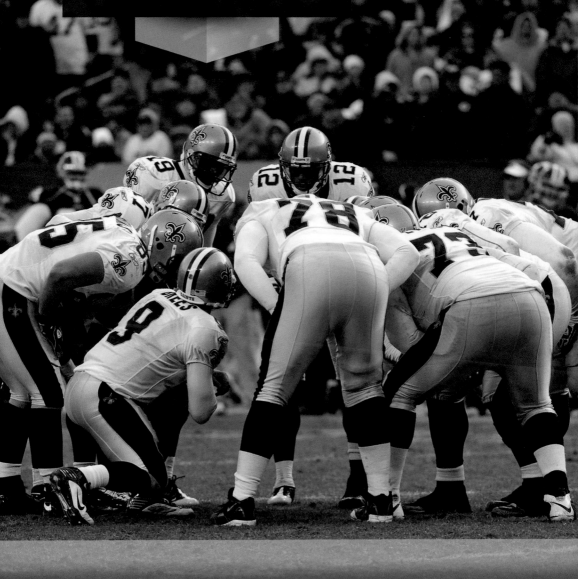

Just like their city, Saints players and fans have special traditions. Perhaps the most well-known is the team's pregame huddle led by Drew Brees.

Brees hollers and his teammates answer. The huddle gets the players fired up to win.

Saints fans love to cheer for the Black and Gold. Many players say the Superdome is one of the loudest stadiums in the NFL.

WHO DAT?

One of the Saints' fan traditions is a famous chant. They yell, "Who dat? Who dat? Who dat say dey gonna beat dem Saints?"

Opponents have trouble hearing one another. For the Saints, the noise means a better home-field advantage!

MORE ABOUT THE SAINTS

Team name:
New Orleans Saints

Team name explained:
Named after All Saints Day holiday and after the jazz song, "When the Saints Go Marching In"

Nickname:
The Black and Gold

Joined NFL: 1967

Conference: NFC

Division: South

Main rivals: Atlanta Falcons, Carolina Panthers

Hometown:
New Orleans, Louisiana

Training camp location:
The Greenbrier, White Sulphur Springs, West Virginia

LOUISIANA

N
W + E
S

NEW ORLEANS

Home stadium name:
Mercedes-Benz Superdome

Stadium opened: 1975

Seats in stadium: 73,208

Logo: A *fleur-de-lis* symbol

Colors: Black, white, gold

Mascots: Gumbo and Sir Saint

GLOSSARY

conference—a large grouping of sports teams that often play one another

defense—the group of players who try to stop the opposing team from scoring

division—a small grouping of sports teams that often play one another; usually there are several divisions of teams in a conference.

drafted—chose a college athlete to play for a professional team

expansion team—a new team added to a sports league

intercepts—catches a pass thrown by the opposing team

offense—the group of players who try to move down the field and score

quarterback—a player on offense whose main job is to throw and hand off the ball

rival—a long-standing opponent

running back—a player on offense whose main job is to run with the ball

rushing yards—yards gained by running with the ball

sacks—plays during which a player on defense tackles the opposing quarterback for a loss of yards

Super Bowl—the championship game for the NFL

wide receiver—a player on offense whose main job is to catch passes from the quarterback

winning record—when a team has more wins than losses in a season

TO LEARN MORE

AT THE LIBRARY

Christopher, Matt. *Drew Brees*. New York, N.Y.: Little, Brown and Company, 2015.

Wyner, Zach. *New Orleans Saints*. New York, N.Y.: AV2 by Weigl, 2015.

Zappa, Marcia. *New Orleans Saints*. Minneapolis, Minn.: Abdo Publishing, 2015.

ON THE WEB

Learning more about the New Orleans Saints is as easy as 1, 2, 3.

1. Go to www.factsurfer.com.

2. Enter "New Orleans Saints" into the search box.

3. Click the "Surf" button and you will see a list of related web sites.

With factsurfer.com, finding more information is just a click away.

INDEX

The images in this book are reproduced through the courtesy of: Corbis, front cover (large, small), pp. 10-11, 11, 18 (top), 26; PCN Photography/ Alamy, pp. 4-5, 16-17, 23 (right); Brian Snyder/ Reuters/ Newscom, p. 5; Scott Audette/ Reuters/ Newscom, p. 7; Jeff Haynes/ Reuters/ Newscom, pp. 8-9; Cal Sport Media/ Alamy, pp. 12-13; Deposit Photos/ Glow Images, pp. 12-13 (logos), 18-19 (logos), 28-29 (logos); Ferd Kaufman/ AP Images, p. 14; Kevin Terrell/ AP Images, p. 15; Al Golub/ AP Images, p. 16; Al Messerschmidt/ AP Images, p. 18 (bottom); Bill Greenblatt/ UPI Photo Service/ Newscom, p. 19 (top left); Action Sports Photography, p. 19 (top right); Ben Liebenberg/ AP Images, p. 19 (bottom); Astrid Stawiarz/ Getty Images, pp. 20-21; David Maxwell/ EPA/ Newscom, p. 21; NFL Photos/ AP Images, pp. 22 (left), 22-23; Otto Gruele Jr/ Getty Images, p. 22 (middle); Focus On Sport/ Getty Images, p. 22 (right); Greg Trott/ AP Images, p. 23 (left); David Drapkin/ AP Images, p. 23 (middle); SportsAge/ Icon SMI/ Newscom, p. 24; Derick Hingle/ Icon SMI/ Newscom, p. 25; Paul Spinelli/ AP Images, pp. 26-27; Tyler Kaufmann/ Cal Sport Media/ Newscom, p. 28; Sean Xu, p. 29 (stadium); Manny Flores/ Cal Sport Media/ Newscom, p. 29 (mascot right); John Korduner/ Icon SMI/ Newscom, p. 29 (mascot left).